Titanic
Bridget Minamore

OUT
SPOKEN
PRESS

First Edition

Copyright © Out-Spoken Press 2016
First published in 2016 by Out-Spoken Press

Design & Art Direction
Ben Lee

Printed & Bound by:
Print Resources

Typeset in Baskerville

ISBN: 978-0-9931038-5-8

Foreword

I first came across Bridget Minamore's poetry as a judge for the 2009 Roundhouse Poetry Slam. Minamore's refreshing take on the world and the way she combined a number of different registers in her writing made it clear to me that she was a poet to watch. In the intervening years, the hybrid quality of those early poems has been carefully honed creating a poetics that is supple enough to be responsive to the contemporary sphere while also pulling off that ancient magic to which all poetry aspires: stopping time to hold a moment still on the page.

The work collected in *Titanic* is both a riff on the common stock of popular culture and a wonderfully unsettling excavation of how it feels to love:

> I want to cut your legs off
> not so you can't walk away,
> more in the hope you'll stay
> exactly where I want to put you. ('Against All Odds')

The stakes here are high because the poet is not varnishing the sentiment to present a glossy version of events. This is particularly evocative because so much of what we know about love, especially what we learn from popular culture, seems to be about conceal-ment. In these poems, we are getting something richer because Minamore shows us the extremes to which love takes us. Crucially, this is writing with a knowledge of what it means to fix a person in language so that the poems explore not just longing but the act of writing. Though words fail us, we write and though we fail each other, we love.

Kayo Chingonyi, Poet.

Contents

Give me just a second and I'll be alright
Surely one more moment couldn't break my heart
Give me 'til tomorrow then I'll be okay

— Daniel Bedingfield

Half Past Five

Her smile was like a fishing net
her hands, hooks
her eyes, a two-seater canoe

but it is me who lies next to you
Here and Now

me who melts in the heat of
your half-clothed body.

Burn The Tapes

I do not know what love feels like

but lust is Ben Kenney's fourth album stuck on repeat
and two bodies too weak to turn it to silence.

Warm It Up/The Yard

White boys with long hair who wear t-shirts three days in a row
Black boys in tight jeans who smell of overpriced cologne
Asian boys with crew cuts grasping last generation iPhones

How many of them will be the ones
to know the sound I make when I

Runnin' Around With You, Tell Me

She arrived like a well-worn speed bump

in the way.

Do I Wanna Know

I'm not sure I know what love feels like
but lust is your arm across from me,
our bodies fully clothed and
a coil from somewhere deep inside,
an overfed snake, a fat cobra,

      waiting to spring

in the dark.

Speakerboxxx

The first time we're challenged
    or confronted
    or whatever you want to call it
is unexpected.

A shock.

A third party neither of us knows that well
glanced for too long a moment.
In hindsight, I can tell she was focused
on the way your hand likes to hover behind
the small of my back
like an unsteady see-saw –
back and forth, back and forth.
In hindsight, her second look is obvious.
In hindsight, I see the cogs turning in her head
as clearly as she saw me, then you
      and then suddenly   us.

Her mouth opened, accent curled around her consonants,
tongue flicking with the recognition of easy prey

are you two shagging each other?

But A Second Hand Emotion

You're an asthma attack
                          you make my lungs tight
                    my chest contract
              my back press against my breasts
my airwaves are a mess.

Against All Odds

I want to cut your legs off

not so you can't walk away,
more in the hope you'll stay
exactly where I want to put you.

Taken Its Toll

You know this
21st century thing
of not defining
romantic
and/or sexual
relationships

it's a bit shit
isn't it?

The Love Below

are you two shagging each other?

Our replies were the epitome
of the bad American romantic comedy
I wish the two of us were starring in.
We said nothing for a beat too long
     and then spoke at the same time
     and then paused
     and then sighed.
I wish I could say I said nothing
because I could feel you were about to answer
or because I trusted you,
but I was just scared I'd start to laugh
     which wouldn't have helped.
But it's funny – really funny –
that was the one moment we both knew exactly
how the other was feeling.

We'd never been more in tune.

I turned quiet and you quipped
with a kitten-joke stuck on your tongue
     she doesn't put out, but I've been trying
so I replied with an unconvincing
     as if.

I had never said the words *as if* before
because I am not a teenager
in a bad American romantic comedy
but in that moment *as if* is all I could say.
She, the third party, raised her eyebrows,

     shrugged,
      ok.

Thnks Fr Th Mmrs

I start taking your lighters to spite you.

Perhaps if your cigarettes couldn't be lit
then your lungs would be clearer
your pores would unblock
and you would come to tell me
how you feel.

Oh Baby, Baby

At the station a busker
sings Britney Spears.

Later on the train
I remember the busker
and burst into tears.

No No No

The blue in your words
is between us now.

It squats on ocean shoulders
and watches us try to talk small,

sits pissing and spitting
in the spaces between each wave.

We're getting shat on every time
we try to have a conversation

and I'm angry you still can't smell it.
It's so rancid I can taste it

on the tip of my tongue, but you
always seem to have a cold.

Your nose is blocked
and my eyes are running.

(Holding On To) The Cracks

What does it mean to be mortified
      I wonder

watching your hand grip hers.

With You Boy

I think of you so much
it's become
embarrassingpainfulsadcringeawfulshithideo
usmonstrousannoyingannoyingannoyingand
crap.

If You Had A Twin

        it's   like

             you

                              dance

across

                    each

           text   message

a tiny

                cartoon   you

        that   yells

I   TO

      USED   SAY

        I

              YOU

LOVE

                        ROUGHLY

      SIXTEEN

           TIMES

        A   DAY.

We Done Fuss and Fight

There is no church here.

Still, you only tell me properly in bed

where everything we say is a confession.

With Every Heartbeat

I don't think we can ever fully love each other.
It's a startling realisation,
one that picks at the tips of my fingers,
pecking at me when you reach to hold my hand.

There's a flock of birds between us now,
a strange swarm of small beasts
beating their wings like broken time
so I stay away from you.

They're mostly pigeons
all grey and sad and dirty
and everywhere,
but it's the others that alarm me most.

A swan called jealousy,
a crow named anger,
a pair of drifting swallows –
boredom and indifference.

Then there's the other bird,
drumming against the windows of the aviary
spitting storms in the saliva of our mouths.
Her name is

the other girl that you've just started seeing.

Fuckin' Problems

If I compare our doomed relationship to a ship that sinks in the middle of the Atlantic, will you finally start to get it? Or maybe that's too straightforward – you've always said I'm a little bit difficult. Maybe I am the ship and you are the iceberg and after crashing into you I sink, and am not found for a very long time. Or maybe we're the passengers – Jack and Rose – an epic I'll survive long enough to never forget you. Or maybe we're actual passengers drowning due to forces far beyond our control; only God could sink the ship we're on. Or maybe it's more abstract – the ship is a 5000-ton lump of emotion balancing badly on a weary sea, maybe in this scenario I am a struggling passenger that escapes and you are a life raft – shaky but constant, and good enough to save me and get me to shore before you collapse with the weight of me, because your support was never meant to last that long. Or maybe I am my own life raft and I can save myself. Maybe I am the Captain who stays with her sinking ship, and you are God. Sinking it. Or I am God who lets the big beast go – it was for the best, it taught everyone a lesson – I don't know. I don't know. But some way, some how, the Titanic reminds me of you.

I Don't Know Why

You tell me you love me properly and I don't reply.

                     We're in bed and I'm facing away from you.

You've never realised I only do this because I'm scared.

                     My eyes are still far too obvious.

You tell me you love me properly and I don't reply.

                     I say nothing and think of water.

808s &

It's like we're playing the oaky-cokey
and our feelings are in a circle on the floor
and we're jumping in and out in and out
in and out and it's exhausting.
In, out, in, out, in, out, like a shitty fuck.
In, out, in, out shake it all about,
we do the oakey-cokey and we turn around
      and we walk away from each other
      we give up on this thing whatever this thing is
      and we don't even end it properly
      or barely say goodbye
      because that's what it's like
      when you both have hurt one another
      more than one too many times,

    that's what it's all about.

    All together now:

        ohhhhhhh, the oaky cokey
        ohhhhhhh, the oaky cokey
        ohhhhhhh, the oaky cokey

        knees bent

        arms up

        let's break up.

All The Small Things

There's something ridiculous about this moment.

Me, watching you with her.

You, ignoring both her, me and everyone else.

Your friends, watching me, watch you with her –
or maybe they're oblivious to me
and are just watching you with her.

I'm not sure which is worse.

Her, watching you, watching you, watching you –
she is constantly watching you,
she is desperate for attention

and

I hate how much I hate her.

But then I realise I must be watching her watching you,
watching her watching you, watching, watching, waiting,
waiting, commiserating. Say it ain't so.
I will not go. Turn the lights off. Carry me home.

Na na na na na na na na na na na na/
na na na na na na na na na na na na

Hey! Hey! You! You!

My jealousy becomes a Michael Bay movie:

sloppier than Spielberg
larger than life
bright colours
bad cuts
tight clothes to catch your attention
a bad plot I can hardly follow
explosions when explosions aren't needed
a hollow but obvious ending
an unknown star that quickly fades away,

and

a sequel in the works
before the first credits have even rolled.

2 Become 1

You are slowly running your hand along my waist
and I am so aware of my breathing and your fingertips
and the hair on your face that skims the inches of my
shoulder blade that I wonder if our bodies
are the same now, or

maybe in the magic space between night and day –
the space only people who have people understand,

maybe at some time before the dawn we were so close
to one another we became the same person
and we either did not realise or we simply did not care.

Leave Right Now

I miss you. I miss your
friendship and your laughter
and your anger and your
crude jokes and your hands.

I miss you and I'm not sure
I miss the two of us together.

Near, Far

The day when the friend you rejected left
you curled up behind me. Gripping
the dip of my waist like a life raft –
wrists motioned heavy against the current of my skin.

It's ok Leonardo,
you promised to hold on, but

I know you had to let go.

Thank You to the following people:

Hannah Vincent and Joshua Idehen for their extensive editing help and honesty. Sabrina Mahfouz for all her encouragement. Out-Spoken Press for publishing me, and Anthony Anaxagorou for his patience, help and occasionally good jokes. Kayo Chingonyi, Kate Tempest, and Inua Ellams for having my back. Anouk Chalmers for making me realise I really did not want this to be a spoken word show, and all of the above for their friendship.

The Hospital Club and The h. Club Foundation for all their support, particularly Suzanne Clode and Margaret O'Keeffe. Matt Charman and Steven Camden for being there at the very beginning. Warsan Shire for always inspiring me. Mia-Sara, Malika and Natasha for coming to the endless spoken word gigs when we were teenagers, and Angharad and Elle for holding my hand when I first read these poems last year.

Sharon Olds, the boys of the past (yes, you), and James Cameron's Titanic for making me understand what love and loss and heartbreak look like. My Mum, Dad, Aunts and Uncles for their constant love (and hopefully for listening to me and never reading these poems – if you do, everything written is all fiction and please never, ever ask me about them).

Daniel Bedingfield, The Weeknd, Ben Kenney, Kelis, Eurythmics, Arctic Monkeys, Outkast, Tina Turner, Phil Collins, Maroon 5, Fall Out Boy, Britney Spears, Dawn Penn, Kate Nash, Sean Paul & Sasha, Rihanna & Drake, DJ Luck & MC Neat, Robyn, A$AP Rocky, Stevie Wonder, Kanye West, Blink 182, Avril Lavigne, Spice Girls, Will Young, Celine Dion, and all the other artists whose songs made up the soundtrack to this pamphlet. Everyone who has indulged the near-constant references to music in my poems over the past few years – I promise, this is the last of it. Maybe.

You. Thank you so much for reading my words – I appreciate it more than you know.

Other titles by Out-Spoken Press:

Out-Spoken 2015
An Anthology of Poetry

A Difficult Place To Be Human
Anthony Anaxagorou

A Silence You Can Carry
Hibaq Osman